THE HOME FRONT

PRISONERS
OF WAR

Fiona Reynoldson

THE BLITZ
EVACUATION
PRISONERS OF WAR
PROPAGANDA
RATIONING
WOMEN'S WAR

Editor: Jannet King
Designer: Nick Cannan
Consultant: Terry Charman, researcher and historian at the Imperial War Museum

Cover picture: The first German prisoners of war to leave for home, in September 1946.

First published in 1990 by
Wayland (Publishers) Limited
61 Western Road, Hove
East Sussex BN3 1JD

British Library Cataloguing in Publication Data
Reynoldson, Fiona
Prisoners of war.
1. Great Britain. German prisoners of war, 1939-1945
I. Title II. Series
940.547241

HARDBACK ISBN 1-85210-976-9

PAPERBACK ISBN 0-7502-0949-6

Typeset by Rachel Gibbs, Wayland
Printed and bound by Casterman S.A., Belgium

CONTENTS

Prisoners of War

It has been said that in 5000 years of recorded history there have been only 227 years of peace. Although this is a difficult statement to prove, it makes the point that men have spent a great deal of time fighting each other.

As long as there have been wars there have been prisoners of war, and the prisoners who spent several years in Britain during the Second World War were just some of the millions of people who, throughout our war-torn history, have been held prisoner.

For thousands of years being taken prisoner often meant death. In some civilizations it meant slavery; in others, prisoners could buy their freedom if they were rich. Some societies treated their prisoners quite well. It usually depended on how much food the victors could spare to feed the prisoners.

'Prisoners are your brethren [brothers]. It is the Grace of God that they are in your hands. Since they are at your mercy, treat them as you would treat yourself.' (*The Koran,* 610–632 AD.)

In Roman times prisoners of war were used to row the galleys.

Time and again in recent centuries, governments have tried to agree on laws to help protect prisoners of war. In 1929, thirty-four countries (but not the Soviet Union) signed the Geneva Convention, which laid down guidelines for how prisoners should be treated. For example:

> 'Prisoners of war are in the power of the hostile power, but not of the individuals or corps who have captured them.' (Article 2 of the Geneva Convention.)
> 'It is forbidden to use prisoners of war for unhealthful or dangerous work.' (Article 32.)
> 'Prisoners of war shall be allowed individually to receive parcels.' (Article 37.)

There were ninety-seven articles in the Geneva Convention, some of them very long and detailed. During the Second World War capturing countries were supposed to follow these articles in their treatment of prisoners, but many of these rules were, in fact, ignored.

Above *French prisoners captured in 1347, during the Hundred Years War.*

Below *A painting from 1866 of prisoners surrendering during the American Civil War.*

The First Prisoners

Britain and France declared war on Germany in September 1939, but for some months very little happened.

'In October 1939 the International Red Cross reported that some of the crew of the German submarines U27 and U29 were in British hands.' (*Prisoners of England*, Miriam Kochan.)

The International Red Cross was based in Geneva, in neutral Switzerland. Throughout the war its agents inspected prison camps on both sides to check that they were being run according to the Geneva Convention. In many cases they were not.

The first prisoners in Britain were housed in two camps. Ordinary soldiers were held at Glen Mill Camp at Oldham, Lancashire (Camp 176), but officers were kept at Grizedale Hall, Lancashire (Camp 1), a stately home which was expensive to run. Some people

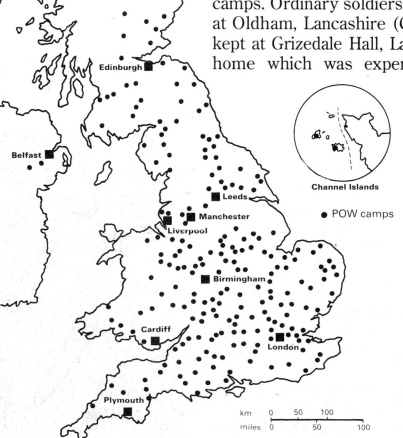

Channel Islands

• POW camps

A map showing the position of prisoner-of-war camps during the Second World War.

Left *The first German prisoners of war at Grizedale Hall in November 1939.*

objected, and one Member of Parliament asked sarcastically:

> 'Would it not be cheaper to keep them [the prisoners] at the Ritz [a luxury hotel in London]?' (Colonel Wedgwood, speech in the House of Commons, 21 November 1939.)

But these conditions were the exception. Most prisoners lived in army huts, barracks and sometimes in tents.

For some time the number of prisoners in Britain was kept down by sending them to distant parts of the British Empire. This saved Britain from having to feed them when food was being rationed. Moreover, at that time, in 1940, the British government feared a German invasion. The last thing it wanted was large numbers of German prisoners in the country who would help the invaders. In fact, because Britain was defeated more often than not in the early part of the war, there were not many prisoners taken!

This situation was to change drastically. The story of prisoners of war in Britain goes from there being two camps in 1939, to a peak of 600 camps, with the final repatriation of the last German prisoners in 1948.

Below *A German airman captured in September 1940, after his plane was shot down over the sea.*

Foreigners in Britain

You never know who's listening!

CARELESS TALK COSTS LIVES

Above *People in Britain were very worried about spies. The government employed artists to design posters encouraging people not to talk about how many ships were in the local port or where their soldier son was being sent to fight.*

Prisoners of war were not the only people held in camps in Britain. In 1939 there were about 75,000 Germans and Austrians in the country. Some had lived in Britain for years. Many were anti-Nazis and Jews who had fled from Hitler's Germany where they had faced imprisonment and death.

When war broke out, some, but not all, 'enemy aliens', as they were called, were rounded up. As far as possible, each person was investigated and put into one of three categories:

> 'Class A or high security risks – 569
> Class B or doubtful cases – 6,782
> Class C or no security risks – 66,002'
> (*A Bespattered Page*, Ronald Stent.)

Most of the people who had fled from Hitler came into the C category.

German spies or fifth columnists (Germans, or German sympathizers, working secretly to undermine Britain) terrified the British government, the newspapers and, therefore, the British people. There

Right *By 1941 many internees were let out of the internment camps. However all 'enemy alien' men between the ages of sixteen and sixty-five had to register. In this way a check was kept on Germans, Austrians and Italians in Britain.*

were strong calls for imprisonment of enemy aliens, particularly in May and June 1940, when the British army were suffering defeats in France:

> 'Round up every enemy alien. However much he or she may profess to hate the Nazi regime the ties of the Fatherland [Germany] prove to be the temptation to betray us.' (*Sunday Chronicle*, 12 May 1940.)

Some people protested against the panic:

> 'It is most improbable that Germany would employ as spies, people who had taken refuge in England.' (Harold Nicolson in The *Spectator*, 26 April 1940.)

Nevertheless, enemy aliens *were* arrested, including the 15,000 Italians in Britain (once Italy came into the war on 10 June 1940). To people who had fled from Nazi Germany, or to people who had lived in Britain for many years, it was frightening and bewildering.

After being interviewed by the police these Italians boarded a coach bound for an internment camp.

Treatment of Internees

Renate Scholem's father was in a concentration camp in Germany. She was in a boarding school in Ramsgate, England, the country to which her family had fled.

On 27 May, 1940 the police arrived and told her to pack a suitcase and go with them. She was not even allowed to phone her mother. She was being interned because she had read some books which the authorities thought were subversive, and because she was living in a sensitive area, near the coast, where she might help invading Germans. She had also been seen talking to a man in RAF uniform (actually her brother-in-law, but nobody believed her). It was thought that perhaps she

Women 'enemy aliens' on their way to the Isle of Man.

was a spy getting information from him.

Renate was taken, still in school uniform, to Holloway prison. Next day she found herself queuing with the other women to empty her slop bucket. They were all internees. One was a nun who had been in a convent in England for twenty years. One was an Englishwoman, married to a German and visiting her family when war broke out. Several were German Jews who had escaped from Germany.

Renate was sent to the Isle of Man, which was being organized to accommodate thousands of internees. Men and women poured on to the island and, not surprisingly, conditions were often bad at first. Some prisoners fell ill:

> 'It has been alleged that many of the interned Italians in England have contracted diseases of the lungs by reason of the bad conditions.' (A letter from the Apostolic Delegator to the British Foreign Office, 17 February 1941.)

Although this complaint was investigated and cleared, there certainly were cases of inhumanity and cruelty in British treatment of internees. This was partly due to bad organization, and partly to panic caused by rumours about spies disguised, amongst other things, as nuns!

Above *A poster warning of the dangers of giving away information to spies.*

Below *The government took over hotels on the Isle of Man to house the internees.*

The Plight of Internees

The worst thing about internment was the isolation: the lack of news and the separations.

Marie and Otto Neurath escaped on one of the last boats to leave Holland the day it surrendered to the Germans:

'At Dover, Otto and I were asked to enter a little booth [very small room] and Otto was taken away. I was suddenly alone in the world.' (*Britain's Internees in the Second World War*, Miriam Kochan.)

In Germany, Nazis were persecuting Jews, but in Britain Nazi Germans were mixed up with Jewish refugees in the camps. It seemed as though the British had no idea of the difference.

'We were just lumped together – Italian waiters, German–Jewish doctors, people who'd lived in Britain

These German–Jewish refugees, arriving by boat at Southampton in 1939, were fortunate in being allowed by the British authorities to stay. Others were turned away and eventually forced to return to Nazi Germany and almost certain death in the concentration camps.

Left *Some 'enemy aliens' were made to do war work. These men, having their tea break, were part of a team clearing up bomb damage.*

for years, people who'd just arrived. The one thing I learnt was to get on with everyone and not to feel bitter. I sat and peeled potatoes with some very interesting people.' (Franz Taubert, Wales.)

Quite soon after the panic of 1940, conditions did improve. One of the internees' complaints was that they were not receiving any post. Steps were taken to improve this state of affairs:

'As soon as he [the visiting bishop] got back to Liverpool, he went straight to the Central Postal Censorship Office, saw the hundreds of unsorted mailbags and protested loudly. Three days later the camp post office was inundated with letters.' (*A Bespattered Page*.)

By early 1941, the invasion panic was over, and gradually more and more internees were released. Many looked back on that time as an education in living. But in some people's eyes it remained a blot on the British record for fairness and freedom.

'No ordinary excuse, such as that there is a war on and that officials are overworked, is sufficient to explain what has happened.' (Major Cazalet, House of Commons, 22 August 1940.)

Below *Hundreds of 'enemy aliens' were interned in a new housing estate called Huyton. In this photograph they are making mattresses out of straw. Nine people lived in each house. Barbed wire surrounded the estate.*

Italian Prisoners

While Britain was worrying about invasion and enemy aliens in June 1940, Italy declared war. In September 1940, Italy and Britain began fighting in North Africa. By January 1941, Britain was winning – to the tune of 130,000 prisoners. The victory was short-lived, due to the arrival of the German army under General Rommel, but some of the prisoners came to Britain.

By the end of 1943 there were 75,000 Italian prisoners of war in Britain, 7,000 of whom were sent to work on farms. (Officers could not be made to work under the terms of the Geneva Convention.)

The Italian prisoners were quite popular with the British people because they often made attempts to be friendly.

'There was an Italian camp just down the road. They loved children and used to make us little wooden toys, carved from any bits of wood they could get hold of.

Italian soldiers captured in North Africa.

Above *These Italian prisoners had to build their own Nissen huts to live in.*

Left *Italian prisoners digging a drainage ditch.*

They'd leave them on an old tree trunk on their way to work.' (Jean Forrest, Glasgow.)

By 1944, Italy was out of the war and the Italian prisoners had more freedom.

'I used to see them at Chipstead, strutting around on Sundays.' (Stuart Robertson, London.)

Treatment of Italian prisoners in Britain and of British prisoners in Italy seems to have been fair. (The British prisoners were each given a daily allowance of wine!)

'As regards spectacles, the Italians agreed to supply them free to any man who, without them, could not read reasonably . . . Our practice was the same.' (*The Work of the Prisoner of War Department*, Foreign Office 1950.)

Below *Prisoners were supposed to receive daily medical examinations.*

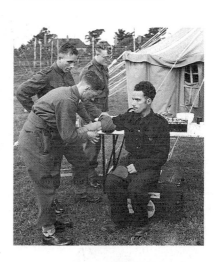

The Italian Chapel

Perhaps the most remote camp for Italians was Camp 60 in Orkney, off the north coast of Scotland. It housed several hundred Italians captured during the fighting in North Africa.

The islands of Orkney are remote and windswept. All the camp consisted of was thirteen army huts in a field. The Italians, however, soon made concrete paths between the huts, and flower beds. They made a theatre in one hut, and a recreation room in another, in which they made a billiard table out of concrete. But the few hundred Italians, far from home in a strange country, still felt that something was missing from their lives and decided to create a chapel.

The British commandant of the camp gave them two Nissen huts. Domenico Chiochetti, an artistic prisoner, started work. He became fired with enthusiasm. Virtually everything had to be made from scrap and rubbish.

Chiochetti collected a small band of helpers – Bruttapasta, a cement worker; Palumbo, a smith;

Above *The Statue of St George, made by the prisoners.*

Right *The Italian Chapel, which was created out of a Nissen hut.*

Left *The inside of the chapel. The commandant of the camp obtained some plasterboard to cover the walls. This was painted to look like brickwork. Palumbo, a wrought-iron worker, made the screen from scrap metal.*

Primavera and Micheloni, electricians; Barcaglioni, Battato, Devitto, Fornasier, Pennisi, Sforza and others.' (*Orkney's Italian Chapel*, Prisoners of War Chapel Preservation Committee.)

Between them they built a beautiful little chapel. The inside of the corrugated iron hut was hidden by plasterboard. Chiochetti painted an altarpiece and went on to paint the whole hut. There was so much work that a painter was sent from another prison camp to help him.

Years later, Chiochetti came back to restore the chapel. By this time it was famous. A service of rededication was held:

Below *Chiochetti and his wife looking at the altar in 1960. The picture over the altar was inspired by a holy picture he had carried throughout the war.*

'Of all the buildings clustering on Lambholm in wartime, only two remain: this chapel and the statue of St George.' (Father Whitaker, 10 April 1960, *Orkney's Italian Chapel*.)

Both were made by the Italian prisoners. Most prisoners found it was better to spend their free time working, rather than sitting around. Building their own chapel was a real inspiration.

Surrender

On 6 June 1944 the Allies invaded France, on their way to defeat Germany. Across northern France the words rang out: 'Hands up! *Hände hoch*!' Sometimes whole armies surrendered, sometimes German soldiers surrendered singly. Hans Reckel was in a trench with other soldiers:

> 'One of the tanks came straight towards us, and directed its machine guns diagonally downwards. All we could do was to climb out and raise our hands.' (Hans Reckel, from *Prisoners of England*.)

A quarter of a million prisoners were captured at that time (30,000 of whom were actually Russians who had gone over to the German side.)

German prisoners captured in 1944.

'We captured far more . . . prisoners than we ever expected, and while it is a great blessing, it is not an unmixed blessing.' (Sir James Grigg, Secretary of State for War, House of Commons, October 1944.)

Prisoners of war found they owned nothing. Often the soldiers who captured them took their fountain pens and watches, although they were not supposed to.

'I had nothing but my uniform. Consequently, when I caught my first cold, I did not have a handkerchief. Through the wire, a soldier from my former company passed a small red handkerchief . . . Our daily diet: tea with milk and sugar twice daily, poured into an empty corned beef tin. If you had one!' (Lieutenant Kurt Bock, from *Prisoners of England*.)

By the end of the war, there were 3.7 million prisoners in British hands. Most were sent home, but half a million were detained, and shared between the British and the Americans. Many sailed for England in the ships that had brought the Allied troops to France.

'On 24 July [1944], on a dull, almost foggy morning, we stepped on to English soil at Gosport. In the streets almost all we saw were women in working clothes, smoking cigarettes, who barely noticed us.' (Hans Reckel, from *Prisoners of England*.)

Above *A German prisoner being arrested by a British soldier.*

Left *German prisoners, who have just arrived in Britain, being marched along an English street.*

Into Captivity

The German prisoners arrived in Britain in large numbers from June 1944 onwards. Many were surprised to be transported in passenger trains, rather than cattle trucks.

'Hours later, a train took us elsewhere. It was not just an ordinary train; we sat on upholstered seats. There was no screaming and spitting at us like in Holland.

Hampden Park: long rows of tables. Interrogation: your name, your rank, your company, your papers. Delousing station. Shower bath . . .

Next day: Nottingham. A huge camp consisting only of tents. Of course, this caused a great disappointment. Here we received cigarettes, a bag and a white handkerchief, which made a great impression on me. But I already had one valuable extra possession: a second blanket . . .

The next camp was Crewe Hall, Cheshire (Camp 191). My first days there I felt only relief at the narrow escape out of hell. And this hell was still going on on the other side of the Channel. My family did not know I was safe and I did not know if my parents were alive. I had already learnt of the death of my younger

Below right A reception camp at Kempton Park racecourse. Prisoners were questioned at these camps before being sent to permanent prison camps.

Below left German prisoners of war arriving in Britain.

brother, Martin.' (Kurt Bock, from *Prisoners of England*.)

German prisoners attending a lecture.

By this time there were camps all over Britain. The following is from a Red Cross report of a visit.

'Camp 197: 5,270 men.
Breakfast: a quarter of bread, margarine, ham, tea.
Dinner: pork with potatoes
Supper: milk, soup, a fifth of bread.'

The same report listed the lessons that had been set up – everything from English (very popular) to shorthand, mechanics, physics and forestry. Football was the main sport, also boxing and wrestling. There were theatre groups and an orchestra. But paper was in short supply.

'Teachers and pupils have shown considerable ingenuity in procuring material (black-out material for blackboards, W.C. paper and the backs of labels for exercise books). (From the Red Cross Report of 24–25 April 1945.)

Prisoners Abroad

As German soldiers were being captured in Europe, other soldiers were nearing release. The prisoners who suffered most were those taken by both sides on the Eastern Front (where the Germans invaded the Soviet Union and were then forced to retreat), and those in the Far East (many of them British). Lack of food and appalling conditions meant many deaths. Of the 50,016 British prisoners of war captured by the Japanese, 12,433 died of maltreatment, disease and starvation.

'So Harry lay on the floor, a wizened up little heap of rag with two claw-like hands and a tuft of dirty hair on

Dutchmen released from a Japanese prisoner of war camp.

his head. "Won't be long now," he said weakly.' (*The Naked Island*, Russell Braddon.)

On the Eastern Front huge numbers of Russians and Germans fought each other. The number of prisoners ran into millions. It is estimated that the Germans took 5.7 million Russian prisoners, 3.7 million of whom died in captivity.

'The encircled Russians put up a fanatical resistance even though for the final eight or ten days they were without food so that they lived off tree bark and roots. When they fell into our hands they were scarcely able to move. The railway network had been destroyed, our own supply resources strained, so it was impossible to save them.' (General Alfred Jodl, Battle of Vjasma, from *Prisoner of War*, Pat Reid and Maurice Michael.)

In such circumstances feeding an army, let alone prisoners, was a nightmare:

'A camp with 20,000 PoWs must cook ten tons of potatoes alone each day.' (Quartermaster of Army Group Mitte, from *Prisoner of War*.)

'The prisoners passed in seemingly endless columns. Those who were unable to continue were shot. We spent the night in a small village and were witnesses of how at night the prisoners roasted and ate those of their fellows whom patrols had had to shoot.' (Dr Faulhaber in the Ukraine, writing about Russian prisoners, from *Prisoner of War*.)

Above left Russian prisoners captured by the Germans. They have been without food or water for some days and are gathered round a hole in the ice.

Above right Russian soldiers surrendering at Kharkov.

Prisoners in Britain

Many British prisoners of war suffered terribly:

'I am five feet nine inches tall. When I was liberated from a Japanese prisoner of war camp, I weighed four-and-a-half stone [28 kgs].' (Private Ankers, Kent.)

In Britain there were shortages, more severe when the war ended, but there was no starvation. Treatment of prisoners was, on the whole, reasonable and fair. Even so, living caged up with hundreds of other men was never easy.

'About eighty men lodged in each hut: apart from the beds, the only furniture consisted of two tables and four benches. Prisoners squatted on the edge of the

German prisoners clearing snow in January 1945.

Above *A German sailor building a model submarine.*

Left *The inside of a prison camp hut, showing the uncomfortable conditions the prisoners lived in.*

bed, or lay on the bunks. There was not a single moment of real peace because one was surrounded by games of cards, stories, discussions, lessons and other noises . . . always the same faces.'(Featherstone Park Camp, summer 1945, *Prisoner of War*.)

There were lectures, concerts, gardening and handicrafts, particularly carving (often of bedposts!). There were jobs to be done in the kitchen and in health care. Camp leaders were appointed who reported to the British commandant about complaints, problems and so on. They also tried to make sure that the prisoners were kept happy. Concentrating on escaping was not a very useful occupation (no prisoner actually escaped back to Germany, although a few did attempt it), so work was often the best way to keep men from becoming depressed.

'Letters from home and making toys to sell kept me sane.' (Hans Jessel, Cologne.)

Below *One of the German prisoners' pastimes was making maps.*

Re-education

With the war over, the Italian prisoners were released, although some chose to stay in Britain and start a new life. Their places in the prisons were filled by Germans, who stayed partly because there was no government in Germany with which to negotiate their return, and partly because Britain was short of labour and the German prisoners were therefore useful. Conditions in Germany were so bad that some prisoners were actually better off in Britain.

Although people began to say that it was not fair on the prisoners to keep them in Britain, there was one other reason for keeping them:

> 'The British were afraid of future wars and were convinced that the aggressive nationalism [desire for one's country to be strong] of Nazism was a German disease. Re-education was meant to give the Germans a chance to see that Nazism had blinded them to real humanity.' (Lieutenant Colonel H. Faulk, from *Thresholds of Peace*, M.B. Sullivan.)

Some of the prisoners were still ardent Nazis:

Many German prisoners, such as these men who are shifting coke in a gasworks in 1946, did work that was vital to the British economy.

Left *German prisoners were made to look at photographs of the terrible conditions inside Belsen, a German concentration camp. This was to show them what had been done in the name of Nazism.*

'Every Sunday at Warth Mills, where 4,000 were packed into an old textile mill, the whole camp stood out in the open and sang the Nazi anthem.' (*Thresholds of Peace.*)

The prisoners had to be taught to accept defeat, and to accept that the government they had fought for had committed terrible crimes against such people as the Jews. Those directing the re-education started by showing to the prisoners films of the opening of the concentration camps in Germany. These camps had held thousands of Jews, gypsies, trade unionists and others who had opposed Nazism.

'No one could look at these pictures without being deeply shocked.' (Hans Reckel, *Prisoners of England.*)

The re-education programme was obviously considered successful, because 123,000 German prisoners, previously held in the USA, were shipped to the UK to be included in it. But perhaps, in the end, the lectures were not as effective as human contact.

'The best re-education for me was being able to talk to ordinary English people.' (John Barnes – a German prisoner who settled in Wales.)

At Wilton Park Training Centre, German prisoners were taught about life in a democratic society. Here, they are producing their own magazine.

Making Friends

The British were not allowed to fraternize (be friendly) with prisoners of war.

> 'Franz and I have now become gardeners. We are set down and off we go whistling merrily. Our lady employer has two dogs which greet us joyfully. The lady looks past us.' (*Prisoner of War.*)

The Germans were still seen as the enemy, but slowly the hatred dissolved.

> 'About four of us always managed to get out of camp. We went to the local pub.' (Alf Eiserbeck, in *Prisoners of England.*)

Officially it was still illegal to speak to prisoners, who missed their families, especially at Christmas.

> 'My dear Mother,
> I received your parcel on 28 December and it was

German prisoners going to watch a West Ham football match in 1947. They wore coloured patches or 'PW', on their clothes to show that they were still prisoners.

28

Left *A British woman marrying a German prisoner of war in 1947.*

put away for New Year's Eve. We were rich! We had biscuits and something to smoke . . . I am all right and have some work to do. A year of monotony would be terrible for anyone who sits around and quarrels with his fate. There are enough of such cases.' (Letter by Egon Schormann, dated January 1947, from *Prisoners of England*.)

After nineteen months of peace, fraternization was allowed at last. The coloured labels on clothes to show the men were prisoners were removed, and in 1947, some of the remaining 59,000 prisoners spent Christmas in British homes.

By the time the last prisoners went home in 1948, they had become farmworkers, decorators, toy makers, piano tuners, roadbuilders and many other things to supplement their small incomes. Some stayed in Britain and married British girls, and many who went home to Germany stayed in touch with the families who had befriended them.

'Then in 1952, came the great day. My wife and I were invited to meet the boys and their families in Düsseldorf. We all had a marvellous time.' (C.V.W. Tarr, from *Prisoners of England*.)

Below *Three German prisoners spending Christmas in a British home in 1947.*

GLOSSARY

Aliens Foreigners

Allies Included Britain, France, the USSR and the USA, who, together, were fighting against the Axis powers (Germany, Italy and other European allies) and Japan.

Concentration camp This term was used in the Second World War to refer to Nazi German camps in which Jews and other groups whom Hitler wanted to be rid of were held, and where millions of people were killed.

Delouse To get rid of lice.

Democratic society One in which the government has been elected by the people.

Fifth column Enemy agents working within another country (spies).

Humane Kind.

Intern To imprison someone because they come from an enemy country.

Internees People who are interned.

Interrogation Questioning.

Inundate Flood.

Maltreatment Bad treatment.

Neutral Not taking sides.

Nissen hut Army hut made of corrugated iron or steel, shaped like half a tube.

Persecute To treat cruelly and punish someone for having certain ideas or religious beliefs.

Ration Only allow people to have a certain amount so that everyone receives a share.

Repatriation Sending someone back to their own country.

Security risks People who are likely to be dangerous to a country.

Service of rededication A church service to make a building holy again.

Subversive books Books that express ideas that go against what a government thinks people should believe.

Take refuge Seek safety.

Upholstered Covered with cushions and cloth.

PROJECTS

1   Make a list of all the things you use and all the clothes you wear in twenty-four hours. Remember to put down everything from pyjamas and toothbrush to library book and carrier bag.

2   Read the poem below and the text on pages 18 and 19. Write out a list of things that you would feel you really wanted to have with you as a prisoner. There must be no more than the number of things in the poem.

> This is my cap,
> this is my coat,
> here is my shaving kit
> in a linen bag.
>
> A tin can is my plate,
> Also my mug,
> I have scratched my name
> on the tin.

This is my notebook,
this is my groundsheet,
this is my towel,
and this is my thread.

'Stock List' by Gunther Eich, 1945.
(From *Thresholds of Peace* by M.B. Sullivan)

3   Find out if there were any prisoner-of-war camps in your area. You could try looking in the local library, a local museum, the local paper, and asking older people or your local history society. Find out as much as you can about the camp – how many prisoners it housed, what nationality they were, how long they were imprisoned for and what work they did. Did any of them stay in Britain after the war?

BOOKS TO READ

Books about prisoners of war

Miriam Kochan, *Prisoners of England* (Macmillan, 1980)

Pat Reid and Maurice Michael, *Prisoner of War* (Hamlyn, 1980)

Ronald Stent, *A Bespattered Page* (André Deutsch, 1980)

Matthew Barry Sullivan, *Thresholds of Peace* (Hamish Hamilton, 1979)

Books about the home front

Nance Lui Fyson, *Growing up in the Second World War* (Batsford, 1981)

Madeline Jones, *Life in Britain in World War II* (Batsford, 1983)

Miriam Moss, *How They Lived – A Schoolchild in World War II* (Wayland, 1988)

Fiona Reynoldson, *War at Home* (Heinemann Educational, 1980)

INDEX

The numbers in **bold** represent pictures.

ACKNOWLEDGEMENTS

The publishers would like to thank the following for permitting us to quote from their publications (listed in the order in which they first appear in the text). Macmillan Publishers Ltd for *Prisoners of England* by Miriam Kochan, 1985; André Deutsch for *A Bespattered Page* by Ronald Stent, 1980; Macmillan Publishers Ltd for *Britain's Internees in the Second World War* by Miriam Kochan, 1983; Laurie for *The Naked Island* by Russell Braddon, 1952; Hamlyn for *Prisoner of War* by Pat Reid and Maurice Michael, 1984; Hamish Hamilton for *Thresholds of Peace* by M B Sullivan, 1979.

The illustrations in this book were supplied by the following: The Hulton Picture Library 7 (top), 11 (bottom), 13 (both), 22, 27 (top); Imperial War Museum 15 (top right and bottom), 20, 25, 27 (top); Italian Chapel Preservation Committee 16 (top), 17 (bottom) (camp photographer, Jas Sinclair); Mary Evans Picture Library 4, 5 (top); Peter Newark's Historical Pictures 5 (bottom), 8 (top), 11 (top); Popperfoto *cover*, 7 (bottom), 9 (top), 10, 14, 15 (top left), 18, 26, 28, 29 (both); Topham Picture Source 12, 16 (bottom), 17 (top), 19 (both), 21, 23, 24. The artwork on page 6 is by Peter Bull Art Studio.